POEMS

KATHERINE MANSFIELD

ISBN: 978-1497398344

CONTENTS

A Day in Bed

I wish I had not got a cold,
The wind is big and wild,
I wish that I was very old,
Not just a little child.

Somehow the day is very long
Just keeping here, alone;
I do not like the big wind's song,
He's growling for a bone

He's like an awful dog we had
Who used to creep around
And snatch at things — he was so bad,
With just that horrid sound.

I'm sitting up and nurse has made
Me wear a woolly shawl;
I wish I was not so afraid;
It's horrid to be small.

It really feels quite like a day
Since I have had my tea;
P'raps everybody's gone away
And just forgotten me.

And oh! I cannot go to sleep
Although I am in bed.
The wind keeps going creepy-creep
And waiting to be fed.

A Few Rules for Beginners

Babies must not eat the coal
And they must not make grimaces,
Nor in party dresses roll
And must never black their faces.

They must learn that pointing's rude,
They must sit quite still at table,
And must always eat the food
Put before them — if they're able.

If they fall, they must not cry,
Though it's known how painful this is;
No — there's always Mother by
Who will comfort them with kisses.

A Fine Day

After all the rain, the sun
Shines on hill and grassy mead;
Fly into the garden, child,
You are very glad indeed.

For the days have been so dull,
Oh, so special dark and drear,
That you told me, "Mr. Sun
Has forgotten we live here."

Dew upon the lily lawn,
Dew upon the garden beds;
Daintly from all the leaves
Pop the little primrose heads.

And the violets in the copse
With their parasols of green
Take a little peek at you;
They're the bluest you have seen.

On the lilac tree a bird
Singing first a little not,
Then a burst of happy song
Bubbles in his lifted throat.

O the sun, the comfy sun!
This the song that you must sing,
"Thank you for the birds, the flowers,
Thank you, sun, for everything."

A Joyful Song of Five

Come, let us all sing very high
And all sing very loud
And keep on singing in the street
Until there's quite a crowd;

And keep on singing in the house
And up and down the stairs;
Then underneath the furniture
Let's all play Polar bears;

And crawl about with doormats on,
And growl and howl and squeak,
Then in the garden let us fly
And play at hid and seek;

And "Here we gather Nuts and May,"
"I wrote a Letter" too,
"Here we go round the Mulberry Bush,"
"The Child who lost its shoe";

And every game we ever played.
And then--to stay alive--
Let's end with lots of Birthday Cake
Because to-day you're five.

A Little Boy's Dream

To and fro, to and fro
In my little boat I go
Sailing far across the sea
All alone, just little me.
And the sea is big and strong
And the journey very long.
To and fro, to and fro
In my little boat I go.

Sea and sky, sea and sky,
Quietly on the deck I lie,
Having just a little rest.
I have really done my best
In an awful pirate fight,
But we cdaptured them all right.
Sea and sky, sea and sky,
Quietly on the deck I lie--

Far away, far away
From my home and from my play,
On a journey without end
Only with the sea for friend
And the fishes in the sea.
But they swim away from me
Far away, far away
From my home and from my play.

Then he cried "O Mother dear."
And he woke and sat upright,
They were in the rocking chair,
Mother's arms around him--tight.

A Little Girl's Prayer

Grant me the moment, the lovely moment
That I may lean forth to see
The other buds, the other blooms,
The other leaves on the tree:

That I may take into my bosom
The breeze that is like his brother,
But stiller, lighter, whose faint laughter
Exhoes the joy of the other.

Above on the blue and white cloud-spaces
There are small clouds at play.
I watch their remote, mysterious play-time
In the other far-away.

Grant I may hear the small birds singing
the song that the silence knows...
(The Light and the Shadow whisper together,
The lovely moment grows,

Ripples into the air like water
Away and away without sound,
And the little girl gets up from her praying
On the cold ground)

A New Hymn

Sing a song of men's pyjamas,
Half-past-six has got a pair,
And he's wearing them this evening,
And he's looking such a dear.

Sing a song of frocks with pockets
I have got one, it is so's
I can use my `nitial hankies
Every time I blow my nose.

Across the Red Sky

Across the red sky two birds flying,
Flying with drooping wings.
Silent and solitary their ominous flight.
All day the triumphant sun with yellow banners
Warred and warred with the earth, and when she yielded
Stabbed her heart, gathered her blood in a chalice,
Spilling it over the evening sky.
When the dark plumaged birds go flying, flying,
Quiet lies the earth wrapt in her mournful shadow,
Her sightless eyes turned to the red sky
And the restlessly seeking birds.

Autumn Song

Now's the time when children's noses
All become as red as roses
And the colour of their faces
Makes me think of orchard places
Where the juicy apples grow,
And tomatoes in a row.

And to-day the hardened sinner
Never could be late for dinner,
But will jump up to the table
Just as soon as he is able,
Ask for three times hot roast mutton--
Oh! the shocking little glutton.

Come then, find your ball and racket,
Pop into your winter jacket,
With the lovely bear-skin lining.
While the sun is brightly shining,
Let us run and play together
And just love the autumn weather.

Butterfly Laughter

In the middle of our porridge plates
There was a blue butterfly painted
And each morning we tried who should reach the
butterfly first.
Then the Grandmother said: "Do not eat the poor
butterfly."
That made us laugh.
Always she said it and always it started us laughing.
It seemed such a sweet little joke.
I was certain that one fine morning
The butterfly would fly out of our plates,
Laughing the teeniest laugh in the world,
And perch on the Grandmother's lap.

Camomile Tea

Outside the sky is light with stars;
There's a hollow roaring from the sea.
And, alas! for the little almond flowers,
The wind is shaking the almond tree.

How little I thought, a year ago,
In the horrible cottage upon the Lee
That he and I should be sitting so
And sipping a cup of camomile tea.

Light as feathers the witches fly,
The horn of the moon is plain to see;
By a firefly under a jonquil flower
A goblin toasts a bumble-bee.

We might be fifty, we might be five,
So snug, so compact, so wise are we!
Under the kitchen-table leg
My knee is pressing against his knee.

Our shutters are shut, the fire is low,
The tap is dripping peacefully;
The saucepan shadows on the wall
Are black and round and plain to see.

Countrywomen

These be two
Countrywomen.
What a size!
Grand big arms
And round red faces;
Big substantial
Sit-down-places;
Great big bosoms firm as cheese
Bursting through their country jackets;
Wide big laps
And sturdy knees;
Hands outspread,
Round and rosy,
Hands to hold
A country posy
Or a baby or a lamb--
And such eyes!
Stupid, shifty, small and sly
Peeping through a slit of sty,
Squinting through their neighbours' plackets.

Covering Wings

Love! Love! Your tenderness,
Your beautiful, watchful ways
Grasp me, fold me, cover me;
I lie in a kind of daze,
Neither asleep nor yet awake,
Neither a bud nor flower.
Brings to-morrow
Joy or sorrow,
The black or the golden hour?

Love! Love! You pity me so!
Chide me, scold me--cry,
"Submit--submit! You must not fight!"
What may I do, then? Die?
But, oh my horror of quiet beds!
How can I longer stay!
"One to be ready,
Two to be steady,
Three to be off and away!"

Darling heart--your gravity!
Your sorrowful, mournful gaze--
"Two bleached roads lie under the moon,
At the parting of the ways."
But the tiny, tree-thatched, narrow lane,
Isn't it yours and mine?
The blue-bells ring
Hey, ding-a-ding, ding!
And buds are thick on the vine.
Love! Love! Grief of my heart!
As a tree droops over a stream
You hush me, lull me, dark me,
The shadow hiding the gleam.
Your drooping and tragical boughs of grace

Are heavy as though with rain.
Run! Run!
Into the sun!
Let us be children again.

Deaf House Agent

That deaf old man
With his hand to his ear--
His hand to his head stood out like a shell,
Horny and hollow. He said, "I can't hear,"
He muttered, "Don't shout,
I can hear very well!"

He mumbled, "I can't catch a word;
I can't follow."
Then Jack with a voice like a Protestant bell
Roared--"Particulars! Farmhouse! At 10 quid a year!"
"I dunno wot place you are talking about."
Said the deaf old man.
Said Jack, "What the Hell!"
But the deaf old man took a pin from his desk, picked
a piece of wool the size of a hen's egg from his ear,
had a good look at it, decided in its favour and re-
placed it in the aforementioned organ.

Evening Song of the Thoughtful Child

Shadow children, thin and small,
Now the day is left behind,
You are dancing on the wall,
On the curtains, on the blind.

On the ceiling, children, too,
Peeping round the nursery door,
Let me come and play with you,
As we always played before.

Let's pretend that we have wings
And can really truly fly
Over every sort of things
Up and up into the sky.

Where the sweet star children play —
It does seem a dreadful rule,
They must stay inside all day.
I suppose they go to school.

And to-night, dears, do you see,
They are having such a race
With their father moon — the tree
Almost hides his funny face.

Shadow children, once at night,
I was all tucked up in bed,
Father moon came — such a fright —
Through the window poked his head;

I could see his staring eyes,
O, my dears, I was afraid,
That was not a nice surprise,
And the dreadful noise I made!

Let us make a fairy ring,
Shadow children, hand in hand,
And our songs quite softly sing
That we learned in fairyland.

Shadow children, thin and small,
See, the day is far behind;
And I kiss you — on the wall —
On the curtains — on the blind.

Fairy Tale

Now this is the story of Olaf
Who ages and ages ago
Lived right on the top of a mountain,
A mountain all covered with snow.

And he was quite pretty and tiny
With beautiful curling fair hair
And small hands like delicate flowers--
Cheeks kissed by the cold mountain air.

He lived in a hut made of pinewood
Just one little room and a door
A table, a chair, and a bedstead
And animal skins on the floor.

Now Olaf was partly fairy
And so never wanted to eat;
He thought dewdrops and raindrops were plenty
And snowflakes and all perfumes sweet.

In the daytime when sweeping and dusting
And cleaning were quite at an end,
He would sit very still on the doorstep
And dream--O, that he had a friend!

Somebody to come when he called them,
Somebody to catch by the hand,
Somebody to sleep with at night time,
Somebody who'd quite understand.

One night in the middle of Winter
He lay wide awake on his bed,
Outside there was fury of tempest
And calling of wolves to be fed--

Thin wolves, grey and silent as shadows;
And Olaf was frightened to death.
He had peeped through a crack in the doorpost,
He had seen the white smoke of their breath.

But suddenly over the storm wind
He heard a small voice pleadingly
Cry, "I am a snow fairy, Olaf,
Unfasten the window for me."

So he did, and there flew through the opening
The daintiest, prettiest sprite
Her face and her dress and her stockings,
Her hands and her curls were all white.

And she said, "O you poor little stranger
Before I am melted, you know,
I have brought you a valuable present,
A little brown fiddle and bow.

So now you can never be lonely,
With a fiddle, you see, for a friend,
But all through the Summer and Winter
Play beautiful songs without end."

And then,--O she melted like water,
But Olaf was happy at last;
The fiddle he tucked in his shoulder,
He held his small bow very fast.

So perhaps on the quietest of evenings
If you listen, you may hear him soon,
The child who is playing the fiddle
Away up in the cold, lonely moon.

Fairy Tale

Now folds the Tree of Day its perfect flowers,
And every bloom becomes a bud again,
Shut and sealed up against the golden showers
Of bees that hover in the velvet hours....
Now a strain
Wild and mournful blown from shadow towers,
Echoed from shadow ships upon the foam,
Proclaims the Queen of Night.
From their bowers
The dark Princess fluttering, wing their flight
To their old Mother, in her huge old home.

Firelight

Playing in the fire and twilight together,
My little son and I,
Suddenly--woefully--I stoop to catch him.
"Try, mother, try!"

Old Nurse Silence lifts a silent finger:
"Hush! cease your play!"
What happened? What in that tiny moment
Flew away?

Grown-Up Talk

Half-Past-Six and I were talking
In a very grown-up way;
We had got so tired with running
That we did not want to play.

"How do babies come, I wonder,"
He said, looking at the sky,
"Does God mix the things together
An' just make it-like a pie?"

I was really not quite certain,
But it sounded very nice;
It was all that we could think of,
Besides a book said "sugar and spice."

Half-Past-Six said--He's so clever--
Cleverer than me, I mean...
"I suppose God makes the black ones
When the saucepan isn't clean."

In the Rangitaki Valley

Valley of waving broom,
O lovely, lovely light,
O hear of the world, red-gold!
Breast high in the blossom I stand;
It beats about me like waves
Of a magical, golden sea

The barren heart of the world
Alive at the kiss of the sun,
The yellow mantle of Summer
Flung over a laughing land,
Warm with the warmth of her body
Sweet with the kiss of her breath

O valley of waving broom,
O lovely, lovely light,
O mystical marriage of Earth
With the passionate Summer sun!
To her lover she holds a cup
And the yellow wine o'erflows.
He has lighted a little torch
And the whole of the world is ablaze.
Prodigal wealth of love!
Breast high in the blossom I stand.

Jangling Memory

Heavens above! here's an old tie of your--
Sea-green dragons stamped on a golden ground.
Ha! Ha! Ha! What children we were in those days.

Do you love me enough to wear it now?
Have you the courage of your pristine glories?
Ha! Ha! Ha! You laugh and shrug your shoulders.

Those were the days when a new tie spelt a fortune:
We wore it in turn--I flaunted it as a waist-belt.
Ha! Ha! Ha! What easily satisfied babies.

"I think I'll turn into a piano duster."
"Give it to me, I'll polish my slippers on it!"
Ha! Ha! Ha! The rag's not worth the dustbin.

"Throw the shabby old thing right out of the window;
Fling it into the faces of other children!"
Ha! Ha! Ha! We laughed and laughed till the tears
came!

Loneliness

Now it is Loneliness who comes at night
Instead of Sleep, to sit beside my bed.
Like a tired child I lie and wait her tread,
I watch her softly blowing out the light.
Motionless sitting, neither left or right
She turns, and weary, weary droops her head.
She, too, is old; she, too, has fought the fight.
So, with the laurel she is garlanded.

Through the sad dark the slowly ebbing tide
Breaks on a barren shore, unsatisfied.
A strange wind flows... then silence. I am fain
To turn to Loneliness, to take her hand,
Cling to her, waiting, till the barren land
Fills with the dreadful monotone of rain

Night-Scented Stock

White, white in the milky night
The moon danced over a tree.
"Wouldn't it be lovely to swim in the lake!"
Someone whispered to me.

"Oh, do-do-do!" cooed someone else,
And clasped her hands to her chin.
"I should so love to see the white bodies--
All the white bodies jump in!"

The big dark house hid secretly
Behind the magnolia and the spreading pear-tree;
But there was a sound of music--music rippled and ran
Like a lady laughing behind her fan,
Laughing and mocking and running away...
"Come into the garden--it's as light as day!"

"I can't dance to that Hungarian stuff,
The rhythm in it is not passionate enough,"
Said somebody. "I absolutely refuse...."
But he took off his socks and his shoes
And round he spun. "It's like Hungarian fruit dishes
Hard and bright--a mechanical blue!"
His white feet flicked in the grass like fishes...
Someone cried: "I want to dance, too!"

But one with a queer Russian ballet head
Curled up on a blue wooden bench instead.
And another, shadowy--shadowy and tall--
Walked in the shadow of the dark house wall,
Someone beside her. It shone in the gloom,
His round grey hat, like a wet mushroom.

"Don't you think perhaps..." piped someone's flute.

"How sweet the flowers smell!" I heard the other say.
Somebody picked a wet, wet pink,
Smelled it and threw it away.
"Is the moon a virgin or is she a harlot?"
Asked somebody. Nobody would tell.
The faces and the hands moved in a pattern
As the music rose and fell,
In a dancing, mysterious, moon-bright pattern
Like flowers nodding under the sea...

The music stopped and there was nothing left of them
But the moon dancing over the tree.

Now I am a plant, a weed

Now I am a plant, a weed,
Bending and swinging
On a rocky ledge;
And now I am a long brown grass
Fluttering like flame;
I am a reed;
An old shell singing
For ever the same;
A drift of sedge;
A white, white stone;
A bone;
Until I pass
Into sand again,
And spin and blow
To and fro, to and fro,
On the edge of the sea
In the fading light--
For the light fades.

But if you were to come you would not say:
"She is not waiting here for me;
She has forgotten." Have we not in play
Disguised ourselves as weed and stones and grass
While the strange ships did pass
Gently, gravely, leaving a curl of foam
That uncurled softly about our island home,
Bubbles of foam that glittered on the stone
Like rainbows? Look, darling! No, they are gone.
And the white sails have melted into the sailing sky...

On a Young Lady's Sixth Anniversary

Baby Babbles--only one,
Now to sit up has begun.

Little Babbles quite turned two
Walks as well as I and you.

And Miss Babbles one, two, three,
Has a teaspoon at her tea.

But her Highness at four
Learns to open the front door.

And her Majesty--now six,
Can her shoestrings neatly fix.

Babbles, babbles, have a care,
You will soon put up your hair!

Opposites

The Half-Soled-Boots-With-Toecaps-Child
Walked out into the street
And splashed in all the pubbles till
She had such shocking feet

The Patent-Leather-Slipper-Child
Stayed quietly in the house
And sat upon the fender stool
As still as any mouse.

The Half-Soled-Boots-With-Toecaps-Child
Her hands were black as ink;
She would come running through the house
And begging for a drink.

The Patent-Leather-Slipper-Child
Her hands were white as snow;
She did not like to play around,
She only liked to sew.

The Half-Soled-Boots-With-Toecaps-Child
Lost hair ribbons galore;
She dropped them on the garden walks,
She dropped them on the floor.

The Patent-Leather-Slipper-Child
O thoughtful little girl!
She liked to walk quite soberly,
It kept her hair in curl.

The Half-Soled-Boots-With-Toecaps-Child
When she was glad or proud
Just flung her arms round Mother's neck
And kissed her very loud.

The Patent-Leather-Slipper-Child
Was shocked at such a sight,
She only offered you her cheek
At morning and at night.

O Half-Soled-Boots-With-Toecaps-Child
Your happy laughing face
Does like a scented Summer rose
Make sweet the dullest place.

O Patent-Leather-Slipper-Child
My dear, I'm well content
To have my daughter in my arms,
And not an ornament.

Out in the Garden

Out in the garden,
Out in the windy, swinging dark,
Under the trees and over the flower-beds,
Over the grass and under the hedge border,
Someone is sweeping, sweeping,
Some old gardener.
Out in the windy, swinging dark,
Someone is secretly putting in order,
Someone is creeping, creeping.

Sanary

Her little hot room looked over the bay
Through a stiff palisade of glinting palms,
And there she would lie in the heat of the day,
Her dark head resting upon her arms,
So quiet, so still, she did not seem
To think, to feel, or even to dream.

The shimmering, blinding web of sea
Hung from the sky, and the spider sun
With busy frightening cruelty
Crawled over the sky and spun and spun.
She could see it still when she shut her eyes,
And the little boats caught in the web like flies.

Down below at this idle hour
Nobody walked in the dust street;
A scent of a dying mimosa flower
Lay on the air, but sweet--too sweet.

Sea

The Sea called--I lay on the rocks and said:
"I am come."
She mocked and showed her teeth,
Stretching out her long green arms.
"Go away!" she thundered.
"Then tell me what I am to do," I begged.
"If I leave you, you will not be silent,
But cry my name in the cities
And wistfully entreat me in the plains and forests;
All else I forsake to come to you--what must I do?"
"Never have I uttered your name," snarled the Sea.
"There is no more of me in your body
Than the little salt tears you are frightened of shedding.
What can you know of my love on your brown rock
pillow....
Come closer."

Sea Song

I will think no more of the sea!
Of the big green waves
And the hollowed shore,
Of the brown rock caves
No more, no more
Of the swell and the weed
And the bubbling foam.
Memory dwells in my far away home,
She has nothing to do with me.
She is old and bent
With a pack on her back.
Her tears all spent,
Her voice, just a crack.
With an old thorn stick
She hobbles along,
And a crazy song
Now slow, now quick,
Wheeks in her throat.
And every day
While there's light on the shore
She searches for something;
Her withered claw
Tumbles the seaweed;
She pokes in each shell
Groping and mumbling
Until the night
Deepens and darkens,
And covers her quite,
And bids her be silent,
And bids her be still.
The ghostly feet
Of the whispery waves
Tiptoe beside her.
They follow, follow

To the rocky caves
In the white beach hollow...
She hugs her hands,
She sobs, she shrills,
And the echoes shriek
In the rocky hills.
She moans: "It is lost! Let it be! Let it be!
I am old. I'm too cold. I am frightened...
The sea Is too loud... it is lost,
It is gone..."
Memory Wails in my far away home.

Sleeping Together

Sleeping together... how tired you were...
How warm our room... how the firelight spread
On walls and ceiling and great white bed!
We spoke in whispers as children do,
And now it was I--and then it was you
Slept a moment, to wake--"My dear,
I'm not at all sleepy," one of us said....

Was it a thousand years ago?
I woke in your arms--you were sound asleep--
And heard the pattering sound of sheep.
Softly I slipped to the floor and crept
To the curtained window, then, while you slept,
I watched the sheep pass by in the snow.

O flock of thoughts with their shepherd Fear
Shivering, desolate, out in the cold,
That entered into my heart to fold!

A thousand years... was it yesterday
When we two children of far away,
Clinging close in the darkness, lay
Sleeping together?... How tired you were....

Song by the Window Before Bed

Little Star, little Star,
Come down quick.
The Moon is a bogey-man;
He'll eat you certain if he can.
Little Star, little Star,
Come down quick!

Little Star, little Star,
Whisper "Yes."
The trees are just niggers all,
They look so black, the are so tall.
Little Star, little Star,
Whisper "Yes"

Little Star, little Star,
Gone--all gone.
The bogey-man swallowed you,
The nigger trees are laughing too.
Little Star, little Star,
Gone--all gone.

Song of Karen, the Dancing Child

(O little white feet of mine)
Out in the storm and the rain you fly;
(Red, red shoes the colour of wine)
Can the children hear my cry?

(O little white feet of mine)
Never a child in the whole great town;
(Red, red shoes the colour of wine)
Lights out and the blinds pulled down.

(O little white feet of mine)
Never a light on a window pane,
(Red, red shoes the colour of wine)
And the wild wet cry of the rain.

(O little white feet of mine)
Shall I never again be still?
(Red, red shoes the colour of wine)
And away over valley and hill.

(O little white feet of mine)
Children, children, open the door!
(Red, red shoes the colour of wine)
And the wind shrieks Nevermore.

Song of the Little White Girl

Cabbage tree, cabbage tree, what is the matter?
Why are you shaking so? Why do you chatter?
Because it is just a white baby you see,
And it's the black ones you like, cabbage tree?

Cabbage tree, cabbage tree, you're a strange fellow
With your green hair and your legs browny-yellow.
Wouldn't you like to have curls, dear, like me?
What! No one to make them? O poor cabbage tree!

Never mind, cabbage tree, when I am taller,
And if you grow, please, a little bit smaller,
I shall be able by that time, bay be,
To make you the loveliest curls, cabbage tree.

Sorrowing Love

And again the flowers are come,
And the light shakes,
And no tiny voice is dumb,
And a bud breaks
On the humble bush and the proud restless tree.
Come with me!

Look, this little flower is pink,
And this one white.
Here's a pearl cup for your drink,
Here's for your delight
A yellow one, sweet with honey.
Here's fairy money
Silver bright
Scattered over the grass
As we pass.

Here's moss. How the smell of it lingers
On my cold fingers!
You shall have no moss. Here's a frail
Hyacinth, deathly pale.
Not for you, not for you!
And the place where they grew
You must promise me not to discover,
My sorrowful lover!
Shall we never be happy again?
Never again play?
In vain--in vain!
Come away!

Spring Wind in London

I blow across the stagnant world,
I blow across the sea,
For me, the sailor's flag unfurled,
For me, the uprooted tree.
My challenge to the world is hurled;
The world must bow to me.

I drive the clouds across the sky,
I huddle them like sheep;
Merciless shepherd-dog am I
And shepherd-watch I keep.
If in the quiet vales they lie
I blow them up the steep.

Lo! In the tree-tops do I hide,
In every living thing;
On the moon's yellow wings I glide,
On the wild rose I swing;
On the sea-horse's back I ride,
And what then do I bring?

Spring And when a little child is ill
I pause, and with my hand
I wave the window curtain's frill
That he may understand
Outside the wind is blowing still;
It is a pleasant land.

O stranger in a foreign place,
See what I bring to you.
This rain--is tears upon your face;
I tell you--tell you true
I came from that forgotten place
Where once the wattle grew,--

All the wild sweetness of the flower
Tangled against the wall.
It was that magic, silent hour....
The branches grew so tall
They twined themselves into a bower.
The sun shown... and the fall

Of yellow blossom on the grass!
You feel that golden rain?
Both of you could not hold, alas,
(both of you tried, in vain)
A memory, stranger. So I pass....
It will not come again

Stars

Most merciful God
Look kindly upon
An impudent child
Who wants sitting on.
This evening late
I went to the door
And then to the gate
There were more stars--more
Than I could have expected,
Even I!
I was amazed,
Almighty, August!
I was utterly dazed,
Omnipotent! Just
In a word I was floored,
Good God of Hosts--Lord!
That at this time of day
They should still blaze away,
That thou hadst not rejected
Or at least circumspected
Their white silver beauty--
Was it spite? Was it duty?

The Arabian Shawl

"It is cold outside, you will need a coat—
What! this old Arabian shawl!
Bind it about your head and throat,
These steps... it is dark... my hand... you might fall."

What has happened? What strange, sweet charm
Lingers about the Arabian shawl...
Do not tremble so! There can be no harm
In just remembering—that is all.

"I love you so—I will be your wife,"
Here, in the dark of the Terrace wall,
Say it again. Let that other life
Fold us like the Arabian shawl.

"Do you remember?"... "I quite forget,
Some childish foolishness, that is all,
To-night is the first time we have met...
Let me take off my Arabian shawl!

The Awakening River

The gulls are mad-in-love with the river,
And the river unveils her face and smiles.
In her sleep-brooding eyes they mirror their shining wings.
She lies on silver pillows: the sun leans over her.
He warms and warms her, he kisses and kisses her.
There are sparks in her hair and she stirs in laughter.
Be careful, my beautiful waking one! You will catch on fire.
Wheeling and flying with the foam of the sea on their breasts,
The ineffable mists of the sea clinging to their wild wings,
Crying the rapture of the boundless ocean,
The gulls are mad-in-love with the river.
Wake! we are the dream thoughts flying form your heart.
Wake! we are the songs of desire flowing from your bosom.
O, I think the sun will lend her his great wings
And the river will fly to the sea with the mad-in-love birds.

The Black Monkey

My Babbles has a nasty knack
Of keeping monkeys on her back.
A great big black one comes and swings
Right on her sash or pinny strings.
It is a horrid thing and wild
And makes her such a naughty child.

She comes and stands beside my chair
With almost an offended air
And says:--"Oh, Father, why can't I?"
And stamps her foot and starts to cry--
I look at Mother in dismay...
What little girl is this, to-day?

She throws about her nicest toys
And makes a truly dreadful noise
Till Mother rises from her place
With quite a Sunday churchy face
And Babbles silently is led
Into the dark and her own bed.

Never a kiss or one Goodnight,
Never a glimpse of candle light.
Oh, how the monkey simply flies!
Oh, how poor Babbles calls and cries,
Runs from the room with might and main,
"Father dear, I am good again."

When she is sitting on my knee
Snuggled quite close and kissing me,
Babbles and I, we think the same--
Why, that the monkey never came
Only a terrible dream maybe...

What did she have for evening tea?

The Candle

By my bed, on a little round table
The Grandmother placed a candle.
She gave me three kisses telling me they were three dreams
And tucked me in just where I loved being tucked.
Then she went out of the room and the door was shut.
I lay still, waiting for my three dreams to talk;
But they were silent.
Suddenly I remember giving her three kisses back.
Perhaps, by mistake, I had given my three little dreams
I sat up in bed.
The room grew big, oh, bigger far than a church.
The wardrobe, quite by itself, as big as a house.
And the jug on the washstand smiled at me:
It was not a friendly smile.
I looked at the basket-chair where my clothes lay folded:
The chair gave a creak as though it were listening for
something.
Perhaps it was coming alive and going to dress in my clothes.
But the awful thing was the window:
I could not think what was outside.
No tree to be seen, I was sure,
No nice little plant or friendly pebbly path.
Why did she pull the blind down every night?
It was better to know.
I crunched my teeth and crept out of bed,
I peeped through a slit of the blind.
There was nothing at all to be seen.
But hundreds of friendly candles all over the sky
In remembrance of frightened children.
I went back to bed...
The three dreams started singing a little song.

The Earth-Child in the Grass

In the very early morning
Long before Dawn time
I lay down in the paddock
And listened to the cold song of the grass.
Between my fingers the green blades,
And the green blades pressed against my body.
"Who is she leaning so heavily upon me?"
Sang the grass.
"Why does she weep on my bosom,
Mingling her tears with the tears of my mystic lover?
Foolish little earth-child!
It is not yet time.
One day I shall open my bosom
And you shall slip in — but not weeping.
Then in the early morning
Long before Dawn time
Your lover will lie in the paddock.
Between his fingers the green blades
And the green blades pressed against his body...
My song shall not sound cold to him
In my deep wave he will find the wave of your hair
In my strong sweet perfume, the perfume of your kisses.
Long and long he will lie there...
Laughing--not weeping."

The Family

Hinemoa, Tui, Maina,
All of them were born together;
They are quite an extra special
Set of babies--wax and leather.

Every day they took an airing;
Mummy made them each a bonnet;
Two were cherry, one was yellow
With a bow of ribbon on it.

Really, sometimes we would slap them,
For if ever we were talking,
They would giggle and be silly,
Saying, "Mamma, take us walking."

But we never really loved them
Till one day we left them lying
In the garden--through a hail-storm,
And we heard the poor dears crying.

Half-Past-Six said--"You're a mother!
What if Mummy did forget you?"
So I said, "Well, you're their Father.
Get them!" but I wouldn't let you.

The Gulf

A Gulf of silence separates us from each other.
I stand at one side of the gulf, you at the other.
I cannot see you or hear you, yet know that you are there.
Often I call you by your childish name
And pretend that the echo to my crying is your voice.
How can we bridge the gulf? Never by speech or touch.
Once I thought we might fill it quite up with tears.
Now I want to shatter it with our laughter.

The Man with the Wooden Leg

There was a man lived quite near us;
He had a wooden leg and a goldfinch in a green cage.
His name was Farkey Anderson,
And he'd been in a war to get his leg.
We were very sad about him,
Because he had such a beautiful smile
And was such a big man to live in a very small house.
When he walked on the road his leg did not matter so much;
But when he walked in his little house
It made an ugly noise.
Little Brother said his goldfinch sang the loudest of all birds,
So that he should not hear his poor leg
And feel too sorry about it.

The Opal Dream Cave

In an opal dream cave I found a fairy:
Her wings were frailer than flower petals,
Frailer far than snowflakes.
She was not frightened, but poised on my finger,
Then delicately walked into my hand.
I shut the two palms of my hands together
And held her prisoner.
I carried her out of the opal cave,
Then opened my hands.
First she became thistledown,
Then a mote in a sunbeam,
Then — nothing at all.
Empty now is my opal dream cave.

The Pillar Box

The pillar box is fat and red,
The pillar box is high;
It has the flattest sort of head
And not a nose or eye,
But just one open blackest mouth
That grins when I go by.

The pillar box is very round
But hungry all the day;
Although it doesn't make a sound,
Folks know it wants to say,
"Give me some letter sandwiches
To pass the time away."

"A postage stamp I like to eat
Or gummy letterette."
I see the people on the street,
If it is fine or wet,
Give something to the greedy thing;
They never quite forget.

The pillar box is quite a friend;
When Father goes away
My Mother has such lots to send,
Far letters every day,
And so I drop them in its mouth
When I go out to play.

The Quarrel

Our quarrel seemed a giant thing,
It made the room feel mean and small,
The books, the lamp, the furniture,
The very pictures on the wall—

Crowded upon us as we sat
Pale and terrified, face to face.
"Why do you stay?" she said, "my room
Can never be your resting place."

"Katinka, ere we part for life,
I pray you walk once more with me."
So down the dark, familiar road
We paced together, silently.

The sky—it seemed on fire with stars!
I said:—"Katinka dear, look up!"
Like thirsty children, both of us
Drank from the giant loving cup.

"Who were those dolls?" Katinka said
"What were their stupid, vague alarms?"
And suddenly we turned and laughed
And rushed into each other's arms.

The Sea-Child

Into the world you sent her, mother,
Fashioned her body of coral and foam,
Combed a wave in her hair's warm smother,
And drove her away from home

In the dark of the night she crept to the town
And under a doorway she laid her down,
The little blue child in the foam-fringed gown.

And never a sister and never a brother
To hear her call, to answer her cry.
Her face shone out from her hair's warm smother
Like a moonkin up in the sky.

She sold her corals; she sold her foam;
Her rainbow heart like a singing shell
Broke in her body: she crept back home.

Peace, go back to the world, my daughter,
Daughter, go back to the darkling land;
There is nothing here but sad sea water,
And a handful of sifting sand.

The Secret

In the profoundest ocean
There is a rainbow shell,
It is always there, shining most stilly
Under the greatest storm waves
That the old Greek called "ripples of laughter."
As you listen, the rainbow shell
Sings — in the profoundest ocean.
It is always there, singing most silently!

The Storm

I ran to the forest for shelter,
Breathless, half sobbing;
I put my arms round a tree,
Pillowed my head against the rough bark.
"Protect me," I said. "I am a lost child."
But the tree showered silver drops on my face and hair.
A wind sprang up from the ends of the earth;
It lashed the forest together.
A huge green wave thundered and burst over my head.
I prayed, implored, "Please take care of me!"
But the wind pulled at my cloak and the rain beat upon me.
Little rivers tore up the ground and swamped the bushes.
A frenzy possessed the earth: I felt that the earth was
drowning
In a bubbling cavern of space. I alone —
Smaller than the smallest fly — was alive and terrified.
Then for what reason I know not, I became triumphant
"Well, kill me!" I cried and ran out into the open.
But the storm ceased: the sun spread his wings
And floated serene in the silver pool of the sky.
I put my hands over my face: I was blushing.
And the trees swung together and delicately laughed.

The Town between the Hills

The further the little girl leaped and ran,
The further she longed to be;
The white, white fields of jonquil flowers
Danced up as high as her knee
And flashed and sparkled before her eyes
Until she could hardly see.
So into the wood went she.

It was quiet in the wood,
It was solemn and grave;
A sound like a wave
Sighed in the tree-tops
And then sighed no more.
But she was brave,
And the sky showed through
A bird's-egg blue,
And she saw
A tiny path that was running away
Over the hills to — who can say?
She ran, too.
But then the path broke,
Then the path ended
And wouldn't be mended.

A little old man
Sat on the edge,
Hugging the hedge.
He had a fire
And two eggs in a pan
And a paper poke
Of pepper and salt;
So she came to a halt
To watch and admire:
Cunning and nimble was he!

"May I help, if I can, little old man?"
"Bravo!" he said,
"You may dine with me.
I've two old eggs
From two white hens
and a loaf from a kind ladie:
Some fresh nutmegs,
Some cutlet ends
In pink and white paper frills:
And — I've — got
A little hot-pot
From the town between the hills."

He nodded his head
And made her a sign
To sit under the spray
Of a trailing vine.

But when the little girl joined her hands
And said the grace she had learned to say,
The little old man gave two dreadful squeals
And she just saw the flash of his smoking heels
As he tumbled, tumbled,
With his two old eggs
From two white hens,
His loaf from a kind ladie,
The fresh nutmegs,
The cutlet-ends
In the pink and white paper frills.
And away rumbled
The little hot-pot,
So much too hot,
From the town between the hills.

The Wounded Bird

In the wide bed
Under the green embroidered quilt
With flowers and leaves always in soft motion
She is like a wounded bird resting on a pool.

The hunter threw his dart
And hit her breast, —
Hit her but did not kill.
"O my wings, lift me — lift me!
I am not dreadfully hurt!"
Down she dropped and was still.

Kind people come to the edge of the pool with baskets.
"Of course what the poor bird wants is plenty of food!"
Their bags and pockets are crammed almost to bursting
With dinner scrapings and scraps from the servants' lunch.
Oh! how pleased they are to be really giving!
"In the past, you know you know, you were always so fly-
away.
So seldom came to the window-sill, so rarely
Shared the delicious crumbs thrown into the yard.
Here is a delicate fragment and here a tit-bit
As good as new. And here's a morsel of relish
And cake and bread and bread and bread and bread."

At night, in the wide bed
With the leaves and flowers
Gently weaving in the darkness,
She is like a wounded bird at rest on a pool.
Timidly, timidly she lifts her head from her wing.
In the sky there are two stars
Floating, shining...
O waters — do not cover me!
I would look long and long at those beautiful stars!

O my wings — lift me — lift me!
I am not so dreadfully hurt...

There is a Solemn Wind Tonight

There is a solemn wind to-night
That sings of solemn rain;
The trees that have been quiet so long
Flutter and start again.

The slender trees, the heavy trees,
The fruit trees laden and proud,
Lift up their branches to the wind
That cries to them so loud.

The little bushes and the plants
Bow to the solemn sound,
And every tiniest blade of grass
Shakes on the quiet ground.

There was a Child Once

There was a child once.
He came to play in my garden;
He was quite pale and silent.
Only when he smiled I knew everything about him,
I knew what he had in his pockets,
And I knew the feel of his hands in my hands
And the most intimate tones of his voice.
I led him down each secret path,
Showing him the hiding-place of all my treasures.
I let him play with them, every one,
I put my singing thoughts in a little silver cage
And gave them to him to keep...
It was very dark in the garden
But never dark enough for us. On tiptoe we walked among
the deepest shades;
We bathed in the shadow pools beneath the trees,
Pretending we were under the sea.
Once — near the boundary of the garden —
We heard steps passing along the World-road;
O how frightened we were!
I whispered: "Have you ever walked along that road?"
He nodded, and we shook the tears from our eyes...

There was a child once.
He came — quite alone — to play in my garden;
He was pale and silent.
When we met we kissed each other,
But when he went away, we did not even wave

To God the Father

To the little, pitiful God I make my prayer,
The God with the long grey beard
And flowing robe fastened with a hempen girdle
Who sits nodding and muttering on the all-too-big throne of
Heaven.
What a long, long time, dear God, since you set the stars in
their places,
Girded the earth with the sea, and invented the day and night.
And longer the time since you looked through the blue
window of Heaven
To see your children at play in a garden...
Now we are all stronger than you and wiser and more
arrogant,
In swift procession we pass you by.
"Who is that marionette nodding and muttering
On the all-too-big throne of Heaven?
Come down from your place, Grey Beard,
We have had enough of your play-acting!"

It is centuries since I believed in you,
But to-day my need of you has come back.
I want no rose-coloured future,
No books of learning, no protestations and denials--
I am sick of this ugly scramble,
I am tired of being pulled about--
O God, I want to sit on your knees
On the all-too-big throne of Heaven,
And fall asleep with my hands tangled in your grey beard.

To L.H.B. (1894 – 1915)

Last night for the first time since you were dead
I walked with you, my brother, in a dream.
We were at home again beside the stream
Fringed with tall berry bushes, white and red.
"Don't touch them: they are poisonous," I said.
But your hand hovered, and I saw a beam
Of strange, bright laughter flying round your head
And as you stooped I saw the berries gleam.
"Don't you remember? We called them Dead Man's Bread!"
I woke and heard the wind moan and the roar
Of the dark water tumbling on the shore.
Where — where is the path of my dream for my eager feet?
By the remembered stream my brother stands
Waiting for me with berries in his hands...
"These are my body. Sister, take and eat."

Very Early Spring

The fields are snowbound no longer;
There are little blue lakes and flags of tenderest green.
The snow has been caught up into the sky —
So many white clouds--and the blue of the sky is cold.
Now the sun walks in the forest,
He touches the bows and stems with his golden fingers;
They shiver, and wake from slumber.
Over the barren branches he shakes his yellow curls.
Yet is the forest full of the sound of tears...
A wind dances over the fields.
Shrill and clear the sound of her waking laughter,
Yet the little blue lakes tremble
And the flags of tenderest green bend and quiver.

Villa Pauline

But, ah! before he came
You were only a name:
Four little rooms and a cupboard
Without a bone,
And I was alone!
Now with your windows wide
Everything from outside
Of sun and flower and loveliness
Comes in to hide,
To play, to laugh on the stairs,
To catch unawares
Our childish happiness,
And to glide
Through the four little rooms on tip-toe
With lifted finger,
Pretending we shall not know When the shutters are shut
That they still linger
Long, long after.
Lying close in the dark
He says to me: "Hark,
Isn't that laughter?"

Voices of the Air

But then there comes that moment rare
When, for no cause that I can find,
The little voices of the air
Sound above all the sea and wind.

The sea and wind do then obey
And sighing, sighing double notes
Of double basses, content to play
A droning chord for the little throats —

The little throats that sing and rise
Up into the light with lovely ease
And a kind of magical, sweet surprise
To hear and know themselves for these —

For these little voices: the bee, the fly
The leaf that taps, the pod that breaks,
The breeze on the grass-tops bending by,
The shrill quick sound that insect makes.

Waves

I saw a tiny God
Sitting
Under a bright blue umbrella
That had white tassels
And forked ribs of gold.
Below him His little world
Lay open to the sun.
The shadow of His hat
Lay upon a city.
When he stretched forth His hand
A lake became a dark tremble.
When he kicked up His foot
It became night in the mountain passes.

But thou art small!
There are gods far greater than thou.
They rise and fall,
The tumbling gods of the sea.
Can thy heart heave such sighs,
Such hollow savage cries,
Such windy breath,
Such groaning death?
And can thy arm enfold
The old,
The cold,
The changeless dreadful places
Where the herds
Of horned sea-monsters
And the screaming birds
Gather together?
From those silent men
That lie in the pen
Of our pearly prisons,
Canst thou hunt thy prey?

Like us canst thou stay
Awaiting thine hour,
And then rise like a tower
And crash and shatter?

There are neither trees nor bushes
In my country,
Said the tiny God.
But there are streams
And waterfalls
And mountain-peaks
Covered with lovely weed.
There are little shores and safe harbours,
Caves for cool and plains for sun and wind.
Lovely is the sound of the rivers,
Lovely the flashing brightness
Of the lovely peaks.
I am content.

But Thy kingdom is small,
Said the God of the Sea.
Thy kingdom shall fall;
I shall not let thee be.
Thou art proud!
With a loud
Pealing of laughter,
He rose and covered
The tiny God's land
With the tip of his hand,
With the curl of his fingers:
And after —

The tiny God
Began to cry

When I was a Bird

I climbed up the karaka tree
Into a nest all made of leaves
But soft as feathers.
I made up a song that went on singing all by itself
And hadn't any words, but got sad at the end.
There were daisies in the grass under the tree.
I said just to try them:
"I'll bite off your heads and give them to my little children to eat."
But they didn't believe I was a bird;
They stayed quite open.
The sky was like a blue nest with white feathers
And the sun was the mother bird keeping it warm.
That's what my song said: though it hadn't any words.
Little Brother came up the patch, wheeling his barrow.
I made my dress into wings and kept very quiet.
Then when he was quite near I said: "Sweet, sweet!"
For a moment he looked quite startled;
Then he said: "Pooh, you're not a bird; I can see your legs."
But the daisies didn't really matter,
And Little Brother didn't really matter;
I felt just like a bird.

Winter Song

Rain and wind, and wind and rain.
Will the Summer come again?
Rain on houses, on the street,
Wetting all the people's feet,
Though they run with might and main.
Rain and wind, and wind and rain.

Snow and sleet, and sleet and snow.
Will the Winter never go?
What do beggar children do
With no fire to cuddle to,
P'raps with nowhere warm to go?
Snow and sleet, and sleet and snow.

Hail and ice, and ice and hail,
Water frozen in the pail.
See the robins, brown and red,
They are waiting to be fed.
Poor dears, battling in the gale!
Hail and ice, and ice and hail.

Printed in Great Britain
by Amazon

61372003R00043